# REMEMBER
## *WHEN*
## *I AM GONE*
## *AWAY*

### Christina Rossetti

*with drawings by Sam Denley*

SOUVENIR PRESS

REMEMBER me when I am gone
away,

# GONE far away into the silent
## land;

$W$HEN you can no more hold
me by the hand,

# Nor I half turn to go

yet turning stay.

REMEMBER me when no more
day by day
You tell me of our future that
you planned:

ONLY remember me;

you understand
It will be late to counsel then or
pray.

YET if you should forget me for
a while

$A$ND afterwards remember,

do not grieve:

FOR if the darkness and
corruption

leave
A vestige of the thoughts that
once I had,

BETTER by far you should forget
and smile

THAN that you should
remember and be sad.

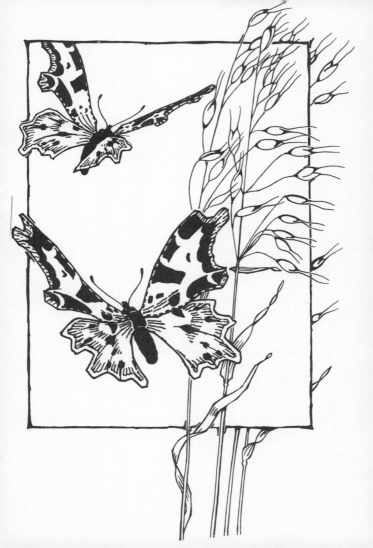

In affectionate memory of
a great actress
JOAN MILLER

First published 1989 by Souvenir Press Ltd,
43 Great Russell Street, London WC1B 3PA
and simultaneously in Canada

ISBN 0 285 62941 7

Photoset and printed in Great Britain by
Redwood Burn Limited, Trowbridge, Wiltshire